Minds Misplaced: Colossians 3:1-2 - And Dispensationalism

ISBN - 978-1937501198

Logo Design: Joseph Vincent

Cover Design by:
Jeffrey T. McCormack
The Pendragon: Web and Graphic Design
www.the pendragon.net

Do Not Set Your Affections on "The Land."

"If then you were raised with Christ, seek those
things which are above, where Christ is, sitting at
the right hand of God. Set your mind on things
above, not on things on the earth. For you died,
and your life is hidden with Christ in God."
(Colossians 3:1-3).

Commentators almost invariably and almost universally, when commenting on Colossians 3:2 and Paul's exhortation to, "set your affection on things above, not on things that are on the earth" make Paul's comments as something almost distinct and divorced from his earlier engagement with the false teachers plaguing the church at Colossae. It is as if in chapters 1-2, the apostle addressed those false teachers but then, in chapter 3 he turns to universal moral *paranesis*, that is not related to that controversy. This view was openly stated by Robertson Nicol: "There seems to be no reference to the false teachers here." (Robertson Nicol, *Expositor's Greek Testament*, Vol. III, (Grand Rapids; Eerdmans, 1970), 537).

A. T. Robertson is another good example of a commentator who "universalizes" Paul's exhortation into something unrelated to the previous polemic discussion: "The Christian has to keep his feet on the earth, but his head in the heavens. He must be heavenly minded here on earth and so help to make earth like heaven." (A. T. Robertson, *Word Pictures, The Epistles of Paul*, Vol. IV, (Nashville; Broadman, 1931), 500).

This has, until very recently, been the position that I have taken on Colossians 3:1f. However, as I have contemplated and examined the actual text, context and controversy, I now wish to make a proposal about Colossians 3:2 that more properly honors what

1

Paul was saying.

To appreciate what I will propose, we must examine the nature of the controversy and seek to identify the false teachers that were plaguing the church at Colossae. It is fascinating to read the literature in this regard.

Before examining that evidence however, it is important to call attention to a simple but important linguistic fact. The word translated as "earth" in Colossians 3:2, in the majority of translations is "gee." This word can speak of the earth as we understand that term, but, it is important to realize that in a huge number of places, perhaps even most, it is better rendered simply as "land." Sometimes, it simply means "ground" (Matthew 15:35).

This word is used some 247 times in the NT. A few random examples illustrates the point:

Matthew 2:6 - Jesus was born in the "land of Judah."
Matthew 2:20 - Speaks of the "land of Israel."
Matthew 4:15f - Speaks of the land of Zebulon."

If the translation of "the land" is followed, this simple, but important change puts a different shade of meaning on Colossians 3:2, one that I think is fully supported by the rest of the contextual evidence. With this in mind, let me turn now to look at the situation in Colossae, to see if we can determine from Paul's polemic against them, which is the better translation, "earth," or "land."

Many commentators tell us that the specific identity and nature of the Colossian controversy cannot be known. Eadie says,

> "There has been no small amount of erudition and research expended on the question, as to what party or parties in Colosse held the errors condemned by the apostle. The attempt has often been made to identify these errorists with some formed and well-known sect. But there is not sufficient foundation for such minuteness. All that we know is contained in the few and brief allusions to their heresies." (John Eadie, *Commentary on the Epistle to the Colossians*, (Grand Rapids; Zondervan, Reprint of the 1957 version), XXX).

McClintock and Strong say, "A great part of this epistle is directed against certain false teachers who had crept into the church at Colossae. To what class these teachers belonged has not been fully determined." (McClintock and Strong, *Encyclopedia of Biblical, Theological and Ecclesiastical Literature*, Vol. II, (Grand Rapids; Baker, 1968), 421). Several suggestions are put forth in this work, including the idea that the Essene theology may play a part in the controversy.

I agree to a great degree with the general comments of Charles Eerdman when he says that: "Some elements of the false teaching are easily discerned. Emphasis was being laid on the ritualistic. Emphasis was being laid upon the observance of sacred days and seasons and upon obedience to religious regulations and forms." (Charles Eerdman, *The Epistles of Paul to the Colossians and to Philemon*, (Philadelphia; Westminster Press, 1956), 19).

3

F. F. Bruce comments on the nature of the controversy:

> "Basically the heresy was Jewish. This seems obvious from the part played in it by legal ordinances, circumcision, food regulations, the sabbath, new moon and other prescriptions of the Jewish calendar. But, it was not the same as the straightforward form of Judaism against which the churches of Galatia had to be put on their guard at an earlier date, a form probably introduced to the Galatian churches by emissaries from Judea." F. F. Bruce, *New International Standard Bible Encyclopedia*, Vol. I, (Grand Rapids; Eerdmans, 1988), 733).

Lenski agreed that the Judaizers were the instigators at Colossae but, he maintained that the brand of Judaizing was different from that in Galatia or in Corinth. (R. C. H. Lenski, *Interpretation of Colossians, Thessalonians, Timothy and Philemon,* (Minneapolis; Augsburg Publishing, 1946), 8f).

The New Bible Dictionary offers this:

> "Some (*e.g.* Hort and Peake) have maintained that Jewish teaching could sufficiently account for all these different elements. Lightfoot argued that the false teaching was that of the Essenes, and we now have considerable knowledge of the Essene-like sect of the Dead Sea Scrolls, though we do not know of the presence of such a sect in the Lycus valley in the 1st century AD. Others have identified

the Colossian heresy with one of the Gnostic schools known to us from 2nd-century writers. We may not label it precisely. Syncretism in religion and philosophy prevailed in those days. We would probably be near to the truth in calling the teaching a Judaistic form of Gnosticism." (New Bible Dictionary, Third Edition, Logos Bible Program).

Contra this view, current scholarship suggests that Gnosticism did not come into existence until the second century. Carl Smith offers this assessment: "The first historically viable gnostics came from Egypt."... "There is no clear evidence presented as yet that establishes the existence of a pre-Christian or even a first century Gnosticism." *(Carl Smith, No Longer Jews,* The Search For Gnostic Origins, (Peabody, Mass; Hendrickson Publishers, 2004), Intro. p. 3). Wright agrees, saying that Gnosticism as a distinct problem in the early church was unknown, and did not become a dominant idea until a century later and in Egypt. (N. T. Wright, *Jesus and the Victory of God,* (Minneapolis; Fortress, 1996), 63).

In contrast to the admission of the Judaizing influence behind Paul's polemic, we find this idea in the *UBS Translators Handbook*:

"The purpose of the letter emerges clearly from its contents. Some people were teaching doctrines in Colossae which were contrary to the Christian message. This false teaching called itself a

5

"philosophy" (2:8), and had, as its core, the belief in "the ruling spirits of the universe" (2:8, 20; see also 1:16, 2:10, 15) who were regarded as intermediary beings between God and mankind, sharing his authority and exercising control over people's lives. So they were to be worshiped (2:18, 23); certain rules were to be kept with regard to food and drink (2:16a, 20–21); and certain religious festival and holy days were to be observed (2:16b)." (Robert B. Bratcher, *A Handbook of Paul's Letter to the Colossians*, UBS Handbook on Colossians, Logos Bible Study Program. Page 2).

They add:

"The Colossian Christians would be Gentiles, not Jews, and it is difficult to assess the significance of the inclusion of the Sabbath in the rules being imposed (2:16) or of the reference to circumcision (2:11). It is significant that there are no OT quotations or allusions in the letter, and that the exposition about the person and work of Christ is made independently of any Jewish expectations about the Messiah." (pp. vi–2).

I would suggest that the only reason that there is any difficulty in discerning the reason for Paul's references to the Sabbaths and circumcision is due to the idea that the author fails to see the

Judaizing movement as the root of the problem, as it was in Rome, in Galatians, in Corinth and in other venues. Furthermore, as Beetham shows, Colossians does in fact contain many echoes of OT prophecy. (Christopher Beetham, *Echoes of Scripture in the Letter of Paul to the Colossians,* (Atlanta; Society of Biblical Literature (SBL) 2008).

As you can see, some commentators agree that there is a "Jewish" (i.e. Judaizing) element to the Colossian controversy. However, they then, based on Paul's warnings against their "philosophy," "angel worship" and "asceticism," insist that the controversy was some hybrid form of the Judaizing doctrine, a strange, perhaps not known form of incipient gnosticism. It is claimed that the false teachers were a strange admixture of Judaism and paganism.

Contra these suggestions, I believe Hort and Peake are correct in their assessment and will seek to demonstrate this. I suggest that Paul's allusions to the nature of the controversy does not suggest a syncrestic Judaism, a nascent form of gnosticism, or a form of paganism. I suggest that what Paul says points us inexorably in the direction of the Judaizers. And if that is true, I suggest that it sheds new light on Colossians 3:2 where Paul urged his audience not to put their affection on the earth.

To help us better understand the nature of the Colossian controversy, we need to look at the things Paul presented in order to combat and refute the false teachers.

☞ **Superiority and All Sufficiency of Christ** – I think it fair to ask: Do we have to look to a syncrestic, quasi-pagan ideology to identify the problem at Colossae? In other words, most commentators look beyond the Judaizing movement to adherents of some form of pagan mysticism to identify those who were claiming that Jesus was not enough and that in addition to Jesus, more was needed. But, do we need to look to pagan mystery religions to find that attitude? I think not.

Look at Acts 15:1: "And certain men came down from Judea and taught the brethren, "Unless you are circumcised according to the custom of Moses, you cannot be saved.""

What do we find in the Judaizing movement? We find the idea that Jesus is Messiah, but, *in addition* to him, the Gentiles need circumcision. Was not the Judaizing movement telling Gentile Christians that they must add Torah and Moses to Christ? Were they not saying that Christ alone was not sufficient, that in addition to Messiah, they needed Moses and the Law, with its New Moons, feast days and Sabbaths? They were teaching the Gentiles that they had to keep the law of Moses, that mandated observing rules about *touching, tasting and handling*, were they not? In fact, the Judaizing movement taught virtually *everything* that Paul combats in Colossians.

Consider the book of Hebrews as it relates to Colossians.

Few commentators would deny that there were two issues at stake in the Hebrews letter. There was the pull of historical Judaism pressuring the letter's recipients to "come back home" as it were, to abandon Christ. However, in addition to that, there is little doubt that there was also the Judaizing movement that accepted Jesus as Messiah, but insisted that one must also keep the Law of Moses and be circumcised to be saved.

Colossians & Hebrews: A Comparison

★ Colossians - Superiority of Christ (Chapter 1) - Creator-Sustainer.

Hebrews - Superiority of Christ (Chapter 1) Creator- Sustainer.

****

★ Colossians - Christ is Superior to the angels - (no angel worship).

Hebrews - He is better than all the angels - "Let all the angels worship him!"

****

★ Contrast with Cultic praxis
Colossians 2 - Temporary nature of the cultus– A Shadow of "good things about to come" (2:16).

Hebrews - The Cultus Temporary, imposed until the time of reformation - A shadow of better things about to come (9:6-10 / 10:1-2)

****

★ Colossians 2:16-22 - The *elements* of the cultic world passing away (*stoichei*).

Hebrews 5:12- 6:1-4 - The readers to leave the elements (*stoicheia*) behind (5:12-6:1-5). The Old Covenant Nigh unto Passing (8:13).

****

★ Colossians 1:12 - Saints anticipating "the inheritance."
 Hebrews - Anticipation of the "eternal inheritance" (Hebrews 9:15 / 11:13f- The Abrahamic Inheritance of *the heavenly land-* Not *terra firma*.

****

★ De-Emphasis on "the land"- as I propose in Colossians 3:1-2.
Colossians 3 - Do not put your affection on the *land*.
Hebrews - You have not come to Sinai (12;18f); We have here no abiding city (13:14).

(You can find an excellent chart by Tom Elseroad, comparing Colossians 1 and Hebrews 1 as each chapter presents the superiority of Christ, at the following site: http://biblelayout.com/doctrine/nt/58_hebrews/Cl1-Hb1-Similar.pdf).

10

These comparisons effectively demonstrate that both epistles are concerned with the identical issues, the same controversy. This suggests that in Colossians, Paul is not dealing with any kind of quasi-pagan mysticism, or, for that matter, even a nascent Gnosticism. He was, just as in Romans, Galatians , Corinthians, and Philippians dealing with the Judaizing movement.

☞ **Philosophy** - The tendency among commentators, especially older ones, is to see here a reference to proto-Gnostics and their claim to possess the true philosophy, the true wisdom. It seems to me however, that this appeal to the "philosophy" of the false teachers as a nascent Gnosticism, or quasi-pagan philosophy overlooks the fact that the Jews very much considered the "Jewish religion" as the true philosophy.

William Hendrickson, commenting on Colossians 2:8-10, notes that in both Josephus and Philo the Jewish religion was referred to as "philosophy." Josephus said that in Judaism, "There are three forms of philosophy among the Jews. The followers of the first school are called Pharisees, of the second, Sadducees, and of the third, Essenes." (William Hendrickson, *New Testament Commentary, Galatians, Ephesians, Colossians, and Philemon*, (Grand Rapids; Baker Academic, 2002), 108+).

It should be kept in mind that Paul's language in chapter 1 lends itself to seeing that he is presenting Christ as the true expression of Wisdom. The ancient Rabbis- in other words, the teaching from Paul's background - wrote of "Wisdom" that was from the

11

beginning. If Paul is drawing on that background and setting Jesus forth as the manifestation and incarnation of Wisdom, then it surely puts his discussion within a "Jewish" context. I will not discuss this further, but Beetham has a good discussion of this.

In addition to this, I think N. T. Wright gives us a possible insight into the source and nature of the "philosophy" and Wisdom that was being disputed in Colossae. Commenting on Colossians 2:8 and Paul's warnings not to be deprived of their inheritance, Wright makes an interesting observation:

> "In other words (v. 8) don't let anyone lead you away captive. But the word Paul uses for 'lead away captive', the very rare word sylagogon: συλαγῶγῶν / συναγῶγῶν ..., seems, like the equivalent words in Philippians 3, to be a contemptuous pun. All you have to do is invert the lambda (in cursive writing) or add a stroke to it (in capitals) and you get synagogon; in other words, 'don't let anyone en-synagogue you, drag you into the synagogue.'" (N. T. Wright, *Paul*, (Minneapolis; Fortress, 2005), 117), 16).

If Paul was, as he often did, playing on the words, this points us directly in the direction of the Judaizing movement. I believe that an examination of the following tenets confirms this.

☛ Traditions of Men

Hendrickson says when Paul warned against the "tradition": "This was not apostolic tradition, nor was it tradition that belonged to the mainstream of Judaism, though it did have something in common with Judaism and embraced the latter's tenets. It was rather a mixture of Christianity, Judaistic Ceremonialism, Angelogy, and asceticism, as verses 11-23 indicate" (2002, 109).

In spite of such attempts to divorce Paul's reference to the "traditions of men" from a Jewish context, it seems better to keep Paul's allusion within just that context. After all, his mention of the observance of "new moons, feast days and Sabbaths," and his discussion of circumcision (2:11f) belong within that context. Why is it felt that we need to isolate, then, his mention of the "traditions of men" from those traditions?

While it is a remote context, we should keep in mind that Jesus spoke against the Jews because they negated the commandments of God by teaching as doctrine the commandments, i.e. the traditions of men (Matthew 15:6ff).

Peter wrote to the righteous remnant of the Diaspora of the ten northern tribes, those who had accepted Christ. He said, "you were not redeemed with corruptible things, like silver and gold, from your aimless conduct received by tradition from your fathers, but by the precious blood of Jesus Christ" (1 Peter 1:18-18). Here is a discussion of the "traditions of men" set firmly within the context of the traditions of Israel.

The grammatical construction of Colossians 2:8-11 lends itself to the idea that verse 11 must be viewed as a response to the claims of the teachers who were offering a greater wisdom and philosophy.

In verse 8 Paul issued the warning against the false wisdom and philosophy. Verse 9 begins with *hoti* translated as "for"or "because" meaning that Paul is now giving the reason why they are to reject that wisdom - i.e. because the fullness dwells in Christ.

Verse 10 begins with "kai" which ties it with the previous discussion of Christ's fullness. The Colossians do not need additional wisdom or philosophy, because they are complete *in Christ*. Thus, *in Christ*, they were circumcised with the circumcision made without hands. This means then, that at least part of the "traditions of men," the wisdom and philosophy that Paul is rejecting and warning about is the attempt of the false teachers to impose circumcision and Torah. The grammatical connections confirms this.

The controversy at Colossians was (partly): "you must be circumcised." Paul responded by telling the Colossians, "you *were* circumcised" but, it is not physical circumcision, received by tradition from the fathers, it is the circumcision of the heart. The connection between Paul's referent to the vain philosophy and the traditions of men, and his insistence that the Colossians had been circumcised, strongly suggests that the traditions he had in mind were the traditions of Judaism.

Thus, Paul's discussion of the "traditions of men" is not an allusion to some pagan philosophy. As Lenski says, "Paul's use of the word (philosophy) does not justify the idea that the Colossian Judaizers had obtained their speculation from the universities of Alexandria, or from some notable 'philosopher' in the technical sense of the term" (1946, 97).

Dunn concurs saying,

> "The already strong implication that the Colossian 'philosophy' was basically Jewish in character is further strengthened by the other items over which the Colossian believers might be criticized or condemned and which we may likewise deduce were central to the Colossian 'philosophy' : 'in the matter of [see BAGD s.v. meros 1c] a festival or new moon or sabbath.'" (James D. G. Dunn, *The New International Greek Testament Commentary, Colossians*, (Grand Rapids; Eerdmans, Paternoster, 1996), 174).

So, for Paul, the "philosophy" and therefore the "traditions received from men," should not be viewed as pagan philosophy. It should be seen as referent to the Judaizing movement that, just as in Romans, Galatia, Corinth and Philippi, sought to impose

Torah on the Gentile believers.

Rudiments of the World

While some commentators see Paul's referent to the "elements of the world" (*stoichiea tou kosmou*) as part of some pagan worship of nature, that view divorces the issue from the other distinctively Jewish elements of the text.

Charles Eerdman noted,

> "The Colossian heresy is further described as being 'after the rudiments of the world.' This phrase probably applies to Jewish ceremonials which the false teachers were attempting to bind on the consciences of the Colossians. Many modern scholars, who find in the Colossian heresy rather elaborate elements of Gnosticism and angelolatry, are inclined to identify these 'rudiments of the world' with the 'elemental spirits' which in pagan and later Jewish belief were associated with wind, cold, heat, and all natural phenomenon. 'The rudiments of the world,' therefore, would mean 'the angelic beings supposed to be in control of the universe.' However, the use of the phrase in Galatians 4:3, and the fact that here it is followed by the references to 'circumcision' (Colossians 2:11, 13) and to feast days and Sabbath days (v. 16,

and also the connection with Jewish 'ordinances' in which the phrase is repeated (v. 20), indicate that it may be sufficient to find in the words a designation of the ritual observances of the Jews. They are here called the 'rudiments' because they belonged to an elementary and preparatory system of religious teaching. They are 'of the world,' belonging to the sphere of the outward and material as opposed to the realm of the spiritual. Such ceremonies and rites were adapted to an age of religious immaturity." (p. 74).

What Eerdman was showing is that there is a consistent flow of thought in Colossians 2. Paul does not jump back and forth between a discussion of pagan mysticism and Judaizing doctrine. His discussion is consistently focused on the Judaizers and their attempt to bring the Gentiles into bondage to Jerusalem and Torah.

It is proper to build on the last comment of Eerdman, as it seques directly into what Paul has to say about those cultic praxis being shadows of the good things that were about to come. In other words, the "rudiments of the world" were the shadows of the better things to come. To put it another way, likewise building on Eerdman, the rudiments were the preparatory building blocks, the foundation if you will, of the coming better things. The problem with the Judaizers was that they refused to "lay aside the elements" and go onto perfection (Hebrews 5:12-6:1-4). (See my

The Elements Shall Melt With Fervent Heat, (Ardmore, Ok.; JaDon Management Inc., 2012) for an in-depth discussion of Paul's use of the distinctive word "stoichiea).

Eerdman was correct to note that in Colossians 2:20 Paul used the term "rudiments of the world" (*stoicheion tou kosmou*), and there can be little doubt that his reference is directly back to verses 14-16- the fundamental "elements" of the Temple cultus. So, if in verse 20 Paul clearly has the Jewish Temple worship in mind, then it is more than tenuous to suggest that in the earlier reference he has something entirely different in mind.

Dunn properly assesses the Jewish focus of Paul's discussion. He notes that the Sabbath was "clearly a distinctive Jewish festival" and that this all but demands, "the probability is that the 'festival' and 'new moon' also refer to the Jewish versions of those celebrations. The point is then put beyond dispute when we note that the three terms together, 'sabbaths, new moons, and feasts' was in fact a regular Jewish way of speaking of the main festivals of Jewish religion." (1996, 175). He continues, "It should be noted that circumcision, food laws, and sabbath were recognized by both Jew and Gentiles as the most distinctive features of the Jewish way of life based on the law."

What this suggests, powerfully, is that Paul's reference to the rudiments of the world, is not an allusion to some esoteric, mystic and pagan influence or doctrine. It was a direct response to the Judaizers seeking to impose the "elements of the world" - the

18

Jewish world, onto Gentile believers.

☞ Circumcision, New Moons, Feast Days and Sabbaths

I suggest that Paul's mention - may I say, focus - on circumcision, New Moons, Feast Days and Sabbaths demands that the central problem at Colossi was in fact the Judaizers. One can speculate about a mystic influence, but, fundamentally at stake was the Judaizing emphasis on Torah observance by followers of Christ. We need to take a look at the tenets that Paul mentions to help us draw our conclusion about Colossians 3:1-2. We will focus mostly on two of those elements: circumcision and the Sabbaths.

In Colossians 2:11-12, Paul tells the Colossians brethren that they had been circumcised with the circumcision made without hands. The reason he tells them this is undoubtedly because the Judaizers were saying, "You must be circumcised and keep the Law of Moses to be saved." Paul responded to this by echoing Deuteronomy 30 and several other OT prophecies of Israel's eschatological restoration, at which time they would be circumcised in heart. In other words, Paul's echoing of the OT prophecies of Israel's last days restoration under Messiah, *when Israel's hearts would be circumcised*, virtually demands that the issue and controversy was Jewish to the core. Modern readers have a difficult time appreciating the importance of those issues and the passion with which they were held in the Jewish mind.

W. D. Davies is certainly correct when he says:

> "To the unsympathetic mind, the observance of the
> Law, centering in the minutea of dietary laws and
> table-fellowship, could not but appear, at worst,
> antiquated superstition, and, at best, annoying, and
> anti-social priggishness: circumcision to such a
> mind could only suggest a barbaric survival. But
> often in history, as for example, the Puritan
> controversy over vestments, great issues have been
> fought in terms of trivia. So in the early church,
> battles for principles often centered around
> apparent piccadilloes. Throughout his treatment of
> circumcision and the Law, remote and pettifogging
> as they may seem, Paul was concerned with a
> central question: the nature and constitution of the
> people of God – its continuity and discontinuity
> with the Jewish people of history." (W. D. Davies,
> *The Gospel and the Land,* (Berkeley; University of California
> Press, 1974), 171).

Why was circumcision such a controversy in the first century? It
is because it was the fundamental and pre-eminent sign of Israel's
covenant with YHVH. While the cultic praxis were part of the
warp and woof of Israel's covenant identity, perhaps nothing else
set her apart like circumcision (with the possible exception of the
Sabbath observance).

20

Christopher A. Beetham calls out attention to the fundamental significance of circumcision in the mind of the Jews:

> "The rabbis of late Judaism taught that circumcision for Israel was foundational for the nation's relationship to God. So important was its implementation that is completion for the male infant overrode the prohibition of work on the Sabbath. They believed that no male who remained un-circumcised - Jew or Gentile - would be allowed to dwell in the world-to-come. Any Jew found to be un-circumcised was liable to the punishment of 'extirpation,' that is, to be cut off from Israel by execution. An un-circumcised male was considered more unclean than even a dead carcass, 'for the foreskin is more unclean than all unclean things' and a 'blemish above all blemishes.' Nevertheless, a Gentile could enter the Mosaic Covenant and become a full member of the Jewish commonwealth as a proselyte through the three rites of circumcision, immersion, and sacrificial atonement (Cf. Colossians 2:11-13)." (2008, 170).

Beetham chronicles that a proselyte could become a full member of the covenant community, by three things: circumcision, immersion and offering of the sacrifices. These are the very three things that Paul addresses in Colossians 2:11-16: Circumcision and Immersion (v. 11-12), and cultic, sacrificial observance. This leads us to believe that Paul is combating the Judaizers who were saying, "Yes, the New Creation has broken in. This is the fulfillment of Israel's hope. So, if you Gentiles want to be full participants in this New Creation, you must be circumcised! You must be immersed. You must keep the sacrificial mandates!" *The issue at Colossi was not paganism.*

It should be observed that each of these tenets were centered in "the land", i.e. *the Land of Israel*, Jerusalem, and the Temple. We cannot fail to remember that in Joshua 5, as the children of Israel came out of bondage, and were ready to enter the promised land, the first generation had died off. The younger men had not been circumcised. As a result, we find this:

> "At that time the Lord said to Joshua, "Make flint knives for yourself, and circumcise the sons of Israel again the second time." So Joshua made flint knives for himself, and circumcised the sons of Israel at the hill of the foreskins. And this is the reason why Joshua circumcised them: All the people who came out of Egypt who were males, all the men of war, had died in the wilderness on the way, after they had come out of Egypt. For all the people who came out had been circumcised, but all the people born in the wilderness, on the way as

they came out of Egypt, had not been circumcised. For the children of Israel walked forty years in the wilderness, till all the people who were men of war, who came out of Egypt, were consumed, because they did not obey the voice of the Lord — to whom the Lord swore that He would not show them the land which the Lord had sworn to their fathers that He would give us, "a land flowing with milk and honey." Then Joshua circumcised their sons whom He raised up in their place; for they were un-circumcised, because they had not been circumcised on the way. So it was, when they had finished circumcising all the people, that they stayed in their places in the camp till they were healed. Then the Lord said to Joshua, "This day I have rolled away the reproach of Egypt from you." Therefore the name of the place is called Gilgal to this day. Now the children of Israel camped in Gilgal, and kept the Passover on the fourteenth day of the month at twilight on the plains of Jericho. And they ate of the produce of the land on the day after the Passover, unleavened bread and parched grain, on the very same day. Then the manna ceased on the day after they had eaten the produce of the land; and the children of Israel no longer had manna, but they ate the food of the land of Canaan that year" (Joshua 5:1-12).

This passage is pregnant with meaning, but, we cannot dwell long here. But, take note of just a few salient points.

☛ Israel was ready to enter the promised land. She was ready to receive the land promised to Abraham (Genesis 15).

☛ Without being circumcised, they could not enter the land– they could not receive the inheritance. Simply stated: *No circumcision, no land!*

☛ When they were circumcised, they entered the land.

☛ When they were circumcised and entered the land, God's miraculous provision of the manna ceased.

☛ When they entered the promised land, they then took of the Passover as a celebration, not only of their deliverance from bondage, but in celebration of deliverance into the land.

In light of all of these facts, for Paul to tell the Colossians that they had been circumcised with the true circumcision, that was the same as saying that the typological meaning of physical circumcision was now being fulfilled; it was "about to be" fulfilled in the better things to which it pointed. It was to say something *radical*. Little wonder that as Hays says, Paul's teaching on circumcision was, "bizarre and scandalous to Paul's contemporaries" (Richard Hays, *Conversion of the Imagination*, (Grand

Rapids; Eerdmans, 2005), 150). Little wonder that Paul called his "circumcision free" gospel, the "offense of the cross" (Galatians 5:11).

E. P. Sanders notes:

> "There is something that is common to circumcision, Sabbath, and food laws, and which sets them off from other laws; they created a social distinction between Jews and other races in the Greco-Roman world. Further, they were aspects of Judaism which drew criticism and ridicule from pagan authors. Jewish monotheism also set Jews apart from Gentiles, but, it seems not to have drawn the ridicule of the pagans in the way that Sabbath, food laws, and circumcision did." (E. P. Sanders, *Paul, the Law and the Jewish People*, (Minneapolis; Fortress, 1983), 102).

Wright concurs with this, observing that several things were viewed as markers, setting Israel off from the nations. He lists the following:

The Land.

The City - Hebrews 13:14.

The Temple - Ephesians 2 / 2 Cor. 6.

The Sacrifices – Romans 12 / Hebrews 13:15.

The Priesthood - Hebrews 5-7.

Distinctive Dietary Laws - Romans 14 / Colossians 2.

Circumcision - Galatians 5 / Col. 2.

Sabbaths and Festivals - Galatians 4 / Colossians 2. (N. T. Wright, *Paul and the Faithfulness of God, (Minneapolis; Fortress, 2013),* 90f).

While Wright notes that other nations certainly practiced many of these things, Israel's practice of circumcision and Sabbaths was very distinctive. He says: "Circumcision and Sabbath, though the former was not absolutely unique to the Jews, were symbols which declared, not least in the Diaspora, 'We are a different people, a people in covenant with the God who made heaven and earth" (ibid, 92).

Life was in the land as Davies says, "There is kind of an umbilical cord between Israel and the land." (1974, 15). He adds, (p. 99): "Life in the land was the seal of divine favor." As Ezekiel 37 shows, to be cut off from the land was to be "dead" and in the grave. John Watts, in his commentary on Isaiah says that to the ancient Jews, "The exiles in Assyria and Egypt are said to have been perishing. But they will be gathered by God to come and worship him on his holy mountain in Jerusalem (v. 13). Separation from the temple is equivalent to death. Being allowed to participate again in Jerusalem is like coming back to life." (John

Watts, Word Biblical Commentary, Isaiah, Vol 24, (Waco; Word, 1985), 344).

Timothy Gray helps us to have at least some insight into how the Jews felt about the Temple and the land:

> "The end of the temple and the end of the world are not unrelated events, according to Jewish and early Christian thought. The temple, both in the OT and Second Temple Judaism, symbolized the cosmos." Much of the architecture and artistry employed in of the tabernacle and the temple's design point to an embodiment of the cosmos. For instance, the molten washbasin is called "the sea" and the altar, "the bosom of the earth (1 Kings 7:23-26). The twelve bulls supported the washbasin were divided into groups of three, each group faced on direction of the compass (1 Kings 7:25, thus signifying the four corners of the world. The seven lamps on the menorah are referred to as 'lights" (Exodus 25:6; 35:8;, 14, 28; 27:20; 39:37; Leviticus 24:2; Numbers 4:9) by the Hebrew word which besides the sanctuary lights is used only in reference to the 'lights' spoken of in the fourth day of creation, where the sun, moon, and stars are also called 'lights." The seven lights were also seen as representing the five known planets as well as the sun and moon. Josephus and Philo both saw the

temple as a symbolic microcosm of the cosmos.....
"If Mark recognized the temple as a microcosm of
the world, then the end of the temple could not be
disassociated from the end of the world– at least
not symbolically. Indeed, what better symbol for
the end of the world than the demolition of its
prototypical representation? This would explain
the reference, in the midst of the discourse, about
the temple's destruction, to the end of the world.
Although these two events seem unrelated to our
modern sensibilities, they may well be closely
associated within the milieu of first century
Judaism." (Timothy Gray, *The Temple in Mark*, (Grand
Rapids; Baker Academic, 2008), 148f).

It is difficult for modern students to fully grasp the connection to
the land and directly connected to that, the Temple, felt by the
Jews. But, it is important that we connect with that feeling and that
passion in order to understand the vehemence of the controversy
that surrounded Paul when he preached his Torah free,
circumcision free, physical sacrifice free gospel.

So, what I am suggesting is that the teachers in Colossi were
telling the Gentile converts that observance of Torah and the
cultus was vital to their salvation. And to say that the cultus was
necessary was to tell them that they must place their hearts and
minds on "the land."

It must not be forgotten in this light that in Messianic prophecy, "the land" is key. All Israel would be "re-gathered into "the land" to serve David their King (Ezekiel 37). But, as Davies suggests, Paul interprets those OT prophecies of Israel's restoration to the land in a manner clearly rejecting a literalistic interpretation of the OT prophecies. He and the other NT writers saw, and affirmed for instance, that the prophecies of the Messianic Temple were fulfilled in Christ and his body (2 Corinthians 6:16f; 1 Peter 2:4f). To state the case simply, if the Messianic prophecies of the temple were interpreted as spiritually fulfilled in Christ and his body, then it is patently obvious that the promises of the land must be interpreted spiritually as well. A spiritual temple does not sit on a literal land. But, if the Judaizers were emphasizing literal temple worship, literal circumcision, literal observance of the cultic feast days, there is little doubt that they were likewise insisting that the Messianic prophecies of the restoration of Israel and the establishment of the kingdom was fundamentally tied to "the land."

If we see, as Beetham well notes, that Paul is indeed echoing those OT prophecies of Israel's last days restoration, when they would be circumcised in heart, it forces us to re-examine the issue of "the land" because in those OT prophecies, Israel would be circumcised in heart when she was restored to "the land." Let me express it like this:

Paul said the "New Moons, feast days and Sabbaths" were, when he wrote, a "shadow of good things *about to come*" (from *mello*, in the infinitive. Virtually all lexicons say that *mello*, with the infinitive has a primary definition of "about to be, to be on the point of." (See e.g. Blass-DeBrunner, *A Greek Grammar of the New Testament and Other Early Christian Literature,* (Chicago; University of Chicago Press, 1961),181). As noted earlier, It is clear that if Paul was echoing Deuteronomy 30 and other OT prophecies of the circumcision of the heart, that he was also seeing physical circumcision as typological, just like all the other cultic praxis.

The fact is that in Paul's mention of circumcision, new moons, feast days and sabbaths, all of these tenets are tied inseparably to "the land." For Paul to say that for those in Christ circumcision (and those cultic observances) was of no value, this indicated to Paul's Jewish adversaries that Paul was saying that the physical connection with Abraham was nullified, the land was forfeited (ignoring the spiritual fulfillment). Such a doctrine struck at the very foundation of Israel's identity as God's chosen people! They were completely failing to see how Paul identified those physical things as the shadows, the types that were now fulfilled - not declared to be failures - in Christ.

To mandate observance of the Sabbath festivals was to demand pilgrimages to the land. After all, in a literalistic interpretation of Zechariah 14 (and other texts) the Messianic Temple was to be in Jerusalem, (cf. Isaiah 2:2f) and if anyone, surely including the

Gentiles, did not go to Jerusalem to worship, they would be cursed (Zechariah 14).

As Wright points out, in Jewish thought, the world hung on three things: Torah, Temple worship, (and thus, the land, DKP) and mercy. (Wright, *Paul and the Faithfulness of God*, Vol. 1 &II, (Minneapolis, Fortress, 2013), 90, n. 59)

Thus, emphasis on the cultus was emphasis on the land. Given this Jewish emphasis on the land, since the Judaizers were imposing Torah and Temple on the Gentiles, they were in fact telling them that their hope was in the land. In saying the Gentiles had to be circumcised and keep the law to be saved, the Judaizers were saying that the Gentiles' hope, their salvation, was in the land. They *had to put their minds on the land!*

As Bruce Longenecker points out, in Paul's rejection of physical circumcision, the apostle was saying something radical, something revolutionary:

> "What Paul has in mind when he envisages the inauguration of a new world is not, of course, the establishment of a completely new physical universe of matter– a world of cause and effect relationships, held together by forces of gravitational attraction at the molecular level. Instead he envisages the establishment of a new realm of existence. It is the sphere of life wholly

different from the 'cosmos' that has been crucified to Paul, a domain where distinctive patterns of life are operative. As his comments in 6:14-15 highlight, Paul belongs to this new world, where different standards apply, different rules are followed, different habits are formed, different ways of life are practised, and a different ethos exists. The world in which he used to live was characterized by many things, one of which was fundamental distinctions between those who were circumcised and those who were not, those who observed the law of God and those who did not. But Paul has seen the death of that world and now lives in a world where that distinction is not applicable." (Bruce Longenecker, *The Triumph of Abraham's God,* (Edinburgh; T and T Clark, 1998), 37).

He adds: "This eschatological perspective has to do first and foremost with the triumph of God, a triumph that is taking place in the establishment of a new world. It is a world where matters of circumcision and un-circumcision are irrelevant." (p. 46). This was absolutely stunning to the Jewish mind.

What Longenecker does not say, that Davies does, is that in Paul's discussion of circumcision and Paul's gospel, the apostle purposely does not discuss the physical land, at least he never suggests that the physical land retained any theological importance. This is stunning in light of the fact that Paul tells us repeatedly that his eschatological hope was nothing but the hope of Israel, found in Moses, the Law and the prophets. If the physical land, the physical temple and sacrificial cultus was the focus of Paul's eschatological hope of the restoration of Israel, then his negation of circumcision, of Temple, of physical sacrifices, of festival observances and Sabbaths is surely strange, not to say self-contradictory.

W. D. Davies addresses Paul's silence in regard to the land: "Paul ignores completely the territorial aspect of the (Abrahamic, DKP), promise." (W. D. Davies, *The Gospel and the Land,* (Berkeley, University of California Press, 1974)178f).

On page 179 he added:

> "In Galatians we can be fairly certain that Paul did not merely ignore the territorial aspect of the promise for political purposes; his silence points not merely to the absence of a conscious concern with it, but to his deliberated rejection of it. His interpretation of the promise is a-territorial."...for Paul, Christ had gathered up the promise into the singularity of his own person. In this way, "the territory' promise was transformed into and fulfilled by the life 'in Christ.' All this is not made explicit, because Paul did not directly apply himself to the question to the land, but it is

implied. In the Christological logic of Paul, the land, like the Law, particular and provisional, had become irrelevant."

Note: I would call attention to what we have observed above. In Paul's negation of circumcision *(not to mention the other praxis mentioned in Colossians 2) for those in Christ,* Paul was - tacitly perhaps, but powerfully - sending a very strong message *about the land!* In this he was following his master, who had some powerful messages about the land.

Gary Burge, commenting on John 15:1-6 and Jesus' claim, "I am the true vine" calls attention to Israel's connection to the land. He cites Psalms 80:7-13 where the Psalmist posited Israel as the Vine transplanted from Egypt to Canaan where they become God's vineyard. Israel was the vine, the land is where they were rooted. (Gary Burge, *Jesus and the Land* (Grand Rapids; Baker Academic, 2010), 53). (For other OT passages that reveal Israel's ideas about the land and their identity as the Vine, see Jeremiah 2 / Jeremiah 5:10 / 12:11f / Isaiah 27:2 / Hosea 10:1).

Burge insightfully continues his comments on John 15:

"The crux for John 15 is that Jesus is changing the place of the rootedness for Israel. The commonplace prophetic metaphor (the land as a vineyard, the people as vines) now undergoes a dramatic shift. God's vineyard, the land of Israel, now has only one vine: Jesus. The people of Israel cannot claim to be planted as vines in the land; they cannot be rooted in the vineyard unless they are grafted into Jesus. Other vines are not true. Branches that attempt living in the land, the vineyard which refuses to be attached to Jesus will be cast out (15:6)... the only means of attachment to the land is through the one vine, Jesus Christ." (2010, 54).

So, when Paul, in his re-framing of Israel's emphasis on Temple, land, cultus and circumcision, he was, as noted, following the lead of Jesus. Those elements that he discussed are so inseparably tied to one another so that when one was discussed, the other was brought to mind.

Davies then says:

"Paul applies to the new community passages from the O.T. applied to the tabernacle and to the future temple in the land: first Leviticus 26:12 and then Ezekiel 37:27; then Isaiah 52:11, which has reference to priests 'who bear the vessels of the Lord,' the whole community being a priesthood; then 2 Samuel 7:14 form the chapter promising that God would make a house for David. The reference to Lev. 26 is particularly telling in 2 Cor. 6:16b." (P. 186).

Finally, we offer this from Davies:

> "The church is for Paul the fulfillment of the hopes of Judaism for the Temple: the presence of the Lord has moved from the Temple to the church....It is easy to conclude that there was a deliberate rejection by Paul of the Holy Space in favour of the Holy People–the church." (188).

Not only were Paul's words concerning circumcision revolutionary, stunning and offensive to the Jews– with dire implications for the attachment to "the land" - his comments that the Gentiles saints were not to be judged in respect to "the Sabbaths" were equally challenging. Not only did circumcision give the Jews the "title deed' to the land, as it were, but, observance of the Sabbath and the Sabbaths, (and needless to say, the Sabbaths were inextricably tied to Temple and land), but, Sabbath observance held an almost equal place of importance. (Virtually all of Israel's festivals, the "new moons, feast days and Sabbaths" were in fact Sabbaths– (Leviticus 23) - and could only be observed properly "in the land" in Jerusalem, at the temple). Thus, the Judaizers, in their imposition of those cultic praxis, were pointing the Gentiles to "the land" emphasizing its centrality in the kingdom of Messiah.

Dunn shares this about the place of the Sabbath in Jewish thought:

> "The sabbath was another Jewish tradition which
> marked out the Jews as distinctive from Gentiles,
> another essential mark of Jewish identity and
> covenant belonging to God (Exodus 31:16-17;
> Deut. 5:15; Isaiah 56:6). Even before the
> Maccabean crisis, 'violating the sabbath' was
> ranked with 'eating unclean food' as one of the
> chief marks of covenant disloyalty (Josephus Ant.
> 11:346). Characteristically Jewish also is the
> practice of referring to 'sabbath' in the plural, *ta
> sabbata*, as here. It is true that the most unusual
> practice of maintaining one day in seven as a day
> of rest proved attractive to sympathetic Gentiles
> (Philo, De Vita Mosis 2:21; Josephus Contra
> Apion 2:282; Juvenal, Satirae 14:96) but a critical
> or judgmental attitude on the subject, as here, is
> much more likely to express a traditional Jewish
> attitude, defensive of identity and covenant
> distinctiveness." (NIGTC, 1996, 174).

E. P. Sanders adds,

> "There is something that is common to
> circumcision, Sabbath, and food laws, and which
> sets them off from other laws; they created a social
> distinction between Jews and other races in the

Greco-Roman world. Further, they were aspects of Judaism which drew criticism and ridicule from pagan authors. Jewish monotheism also set Jews apart from Gentiles, but, it seems not to have drawn the ridicule of the pagans in the way that Sabbath, food laws, and circumcision did." (E. P. Sanders, Paul, the Law and the Jewish People, (Minneapolis, Fortress, 1983)102).

So, when Paul told the Gentile brethren not to be judged in regard to circumcision or the Sabbaths, this was saying that their identity in Christ was not an identity with the Old Covenant things of Israel. Physical circumcision belonged to the Old Covenant world and age. Circumcision of the heart, as Longenecker noted above, has to with the New Creation that was promised in the Tanakh. When Paul said they had been circumcised with the circumcision of the heart, this was a shocking blow against what we today would call "Zionism" for it meant that their (Gentile) identity was not in "the land" and the Old Covenant cultic observances, but, in Christ and the Torah free Gospel. The Davidic kingdom of which they were now members, into which they had been translated, (Colossians 1:13) *was not based in, or identified with physical circumcision, the temple, the physical sacrifices, the Feast Days— i.e. the land!* It was heavenly (Colossians 3:1-3).

Keep in mind that in Israel's history, it was failure to keep her Sabbaths that led directly to her being led off into Babylonian captivity.

Ezekiel 20: 23-26:

> "Also I raised My hand in an oath to those in the wilderness, that I would scatter them among the Gentiles and disperse them throughout the countries, 24 because they had not executed My judgments, but had despised My statutes, profaned My Sabbaths, and their eyes were fixed on their fathers' idols. 25 "Therefore I also gave them up to statutes that were not good, and judgments by which they could not live; 26 and I pronounced them unclean because of their ritual gifts, in that they caused all their firstborn to pass through the fire, that I might make them desolate and that they might know that I am the Lord."'

From God's perspective, Israel's abuse of the Sabbath extended all the way back to her wilderness wanderings and was virtually continuous throughout her history. And as a direct result of her refusal to honor those Sabbaths, (along with their idolatrous, adulterous ways) YHVH said He would remove them from the land. This was fulfilled in the Babylonian captivity:

> "Therefore He brought against them the king of the Chaldeans, who killed their young men with the sword in the house of their sanctuary, and had no

compassion on young man or virgin, on the aged or the weak; He gave them all into his hand. 18 And all the articles from the house of God, great and small, the treasures of the house of the Lord, and the treasures of the king and of his leaders, all these he took to Babylon. 19 Then they burned the house of God, broke down the wall of Jerusalem, burned all its palaces with fire, and destroyed all its precious possessions. 20 And those who escaped from the sword he carried away to Babylon, where they became servants to him and his sons until the rule of the kingdom of Persia, 21 to fulfill the word of the Lord by the mouth of Jeremiah, until the land had enjoyed her Sabbaths. As long as she lay desolate she kept Sabbath, to fulfill seventy years" (2 Chronicles 36:17-21).

So, just as it was with circumcision, observance of the Sabbaths, all of the Sabbaths, - i.e. the New Moons, Feast days and Sabbaths of Colossians 2:16 - was fundamentally important for Israel to live in the land. (See Leviticus 26). Thus, the conflict in Colossians, focused as it was on circumcision, New Moons, Feast days, Sabbaths and Israel's distinctive dietary laws, *was a dispute about the nature and identity of the Kingdom - just as in Romans 14:17 and other passages. It was a question of whether the kingdom remained centered on the Temple and the Land.* Paul's rejection of everything that was Temple centered was thereby a re-definition of Temple, Land, sacrifices, circumcision!

It is impossible, in Jewish thought, to divorce any of these elements from on another. As Westerners we often create false divisions and distinctions between some of these tenets, but, that is not the Hebraic way of thinking.

Wright notes for instance that in Jewish thought the Temple was inextricably tied to the Davidic kingdom. (2013, 97+). He adds: "It is highly significant for our understanding of Paul, and his re-use of the Temple motif at various key points, that Temple and (Davidic) Messiahship go hand in hand." (P. 104).

So, to reiterate our point from above, the controversy in Colossians was not simply about some arcane dietary laws, or circumcision divorced from the broader matrix of Hebriac thought. Everything that Paul mentions would have been linked in the Jewish mind to the Temple, the kingdom, the land. The false teachers were telling the Gentile converts that they had no hope apart from the observation of the cultus of Torah, circumcision and immersion into the Abrahamic covenant people, obedience to the distinctive laws "touch not, taste not, handle not." They had to keep the Law of Moses to be saved. They had to set their minds on the land.

☛ **Worship of Angels**– This tenet, perhaps more than any of the others, has caused the commentators to look beyond the Judaizing movement and to try to find some pagan source, or, at the least, a hybrid form of syncrestic Judaism. I do not believe this is necessary.

It seems to me that we have sufficient Biblical evidence to suggest that there was an element in Judaism that exalted the angels to such an extent that when presenting the story of Jesus as Messiah, the NT writers felt compelled to contrast him with the angels. This is particularly true in Hebrews, in which the underlying, dominant theme is that Jesus is "better." What is so significant is that the author begins that lengthy epistle with a contrast between Jesus and the angels! To bring this into focus, we need to look at the entire first chapter of Hebrews:

> "God, who at various times and in various ways spoke in time past to the fathers by the prophets, has in these last days spoken to us by His Son, whom He has appointed heir of all things, through whom also He made the worlds; who being the brightness of His glory and the express image of His person, and upholding all things by the word of His power, when He had by Himself purged our sins, sat down at the right hand of the Majesty on high, having become so much better than the angels, as He has by inheritance obtained a more excellent name than they. For to which of the angels did He ever say: "You are My Son, Today I have begotten You"? And again: "I will be to

Him a Father, And He shall be to Me a Son"? But when He again brings the firstborn into the world, He says: "Let all the angels of God worship Him." And of the angels He says: "Who makes His angels spirits And His ministers a flame of fire." But to the Son He says: "Your throne, O God, is forever and ever; A scepter of righteousness is the scepter of Your kingdom. You have loved righteousness and hated lawlessness; Therefore God, Your God, has anointed You With the oil of gladness more than Your companions." And: "You, Lord, in the beginning laid the foundation of the earth, And the heavens are the work of Your hands. They will perish, but You remain; And they will all grow old like a garment; Like a cloak You will fold them up, And they will be changed. But You are the same, And Your years will not fail." But to which of the angels has He ever said: "Sit at My right hand, Till I make Your enemies Your footstool"? Are they not all ministering spirits sent forth to minister for those who will inherit salvation?"

The contrasts here are striking.

Jesus has a better name than the angels.

Jesus is the Son of God, the angels are not.

Jesus is Creator, angels are created.

Jesus is eternal, the angels are created.

Jesus is the source of redemption, the angels administer salvation.

Jesus is God, the angels are servants.

Jesus is King, angels are servants.

The question needs to be asked, if there was not some appeal being made about the importance of angels, why would the author of Hebrews spend so much ink setting Jesus forth as better than the angels? We know that it was common for Jewish writers and speakers to refer to the fact that Torah was given by the agency of angels (Acts 7:53). Paul himself draws attention to this (Galatians 3:19) in an epistle dealing with the same issues as Colossians. So, there is no question that to the Jewish mind, angels were, at least on some level, revered for their role in delivering Torah – which of course was at the heart of the Colossian controversy.

Taken in light of the other tenets that Paul sets forth, I think it untenable to suggest that Paul was discussing some pagan worship of angels. His mention of the angels is a continuation of setting forth Jesus as all sufficient, in contrast to Torah that had been delivered by angels.

Charles Talbert demonstrates from a variety of ancient sources that the Jews did indeed venerate angels. He takes note of Philo and other first century Jews that mentioned angel worship among the Jews.[1]

Not only that, in Deuteronomy 4:19 Moses warned Israel:

> "Take heed, lest you lift your eyes to heaven, and when you see the sun, the moon, and the stars, all the host of heaven, you feel driven to worship them and serve them, which the Lord your God has given to all the peoples under the whole heaven as a heritage." (See also Deuteronomy 17:3 / Jeremiah 8:2).

So, as far back as Moses and into the time of the prophets, there was the reality, the fear of and the mandate against the worshiping of angels by Israel. It certainly should not be strange therefore, if that was a problem in the first century (Philo was a first century Jew).

I think Lenski is correct: "The supposition that they advocated the worship of angels and thus in Gnostic fashion elevated angels rests on a strained interpretation of 2:18." (1946, P. 10). He is right to

---

[1] Charles Talbert, *Ephesians and Colossians, Paideia Commentaries on the New Testament*(Grand Rapids; Baker Academic), 218.

reject a Gnostic influence, but, I see little evidence to suggest that the "worshiping of angels" was not a genuine "Jewish" issue and one incorporated into the Judaizing movement.

I would add that some relatively recent archaeological finds have shed some additional potential light on this issue as well. A 1300 year old mummy revealed a tatoo of Michael the Arch-Angel on the inner thigh of female. It is believed that she was a Christian. In the article, it is stated that in addition to Christians wearing such tatoos:

"Jews of antiquity were fascinated by the identity and nature of angels."(http://www.foxnews.com/science/2014/03/26/scientists-unearth-new-secrets-from-ancient-mummy/?intcmp=obinsite).

So, if we consider the legislation in Torah that forbad Israel from worshiping angels, if we consider the rabbinic evidence, if we consider the historical evidence and even the modern archaeological evidence, it would appear that there is no firm reason for rejecting the idea, the possibility, that the worshiping of angels was a first century Jewish practice that was now being imposed by the Judaizers.

☛ **"Asceticism" - "Touch Not, Taste Not, Handle Not"**

Commentators are, it seems, somewhat quick to appeal to Colossians 2:21 as a form of nascent ascetic Gnosticism. It is seen as a philosophy of self-deprivation and antipathy toward the created order. (See Eerdman, 1966, 19). As a result, it is then claimed that the form of Judaizing teaching in Colossae is distinguished from that which manifested itself in Rome, Galatia, and Corinth. I believe this is misguided and fails to consider the nature of Judaism itself.

Other commentators, while not necessarily positing a pagan source of the controversy, seek to divorce it from the "normal" Judaizing controversy. Dunn cites George Caird who said: "This asceticism is the product of an exaggerated and puritanical form of Judaism." (1996, 175, n. 9). I am not convinced that one needs to look beyond the normal beliefs within Judaism to find the very issues at work in Colossians.

In fact, Judaism was demonstrated, was marked off, in many ways, by the maxim "touch not, taste not, handle not." As Talbert says, among Jews in the first century, "These two things, Sabbath observance and proper food, were public means of identification of Jews in Mediterranean antiquity" (2007, 217- Wright and others have called attention to the fact that *circumcision*, Sabbath and the dietary laws were the Jewish distinctives).

Talbert also shows that according to Josephus, "the two chief marks of covenant disloyalty was violating the Sabbath and eating unclean food" (2007, 215). I suggest therefore that a focus on the covenant was part and parcel of the Judaizing movement and message. The Gentiles had to "keep the law of Moses and be circumcised to be saved."

A quick perusal of some of the laws in Torah as they related to touching and tasting demonstrates this.

There were laws against touching anything considered unclean.

The Jews were not to touch the carcass of a pig (Leviticus 11:8f).

A menstruous woman was not to touch anything that was clean and holy (Leviticus 12).

In cases of flagrant sin, punished by the congregation, nothing that even belonged to the guilty parties was to be touched (Numbers 16).

A summary of YHVH's instructions for Israel concerning unclean things may be found in Leviticus 7:21:

> "Moreover the person who touches any unclean thing, such as human uncleanness, an unclean animal, or any abominable unclean thing, and who eats the flesh of the sacrifice of the peace offering that belongs to the Lord, that person shall be cut off from his people.'"

Here is a succinct summary of, "Touch not, taste not, handle not."

Just read Leviticus 11 to see a list of things that Israel was forbidden to touch or to taste. It may not be too much to say, that in some regards, "touch not, taste not, handle not" is a succinct way of saying "Keep Torah!" It was not "asceticism" as defined and practiced by the mystic pagan cults or at a later time by the Gnostics.

Remember that part of the premise behind the "washing of hands" was related to the idea that the Jews were not to touch or handle certain things. It was fundamentally a part of their religion.

We cannot fail to remember Peter in Acts 10. When the Lord commanded him to eat of the foods / animals in the vision, Peter vehemently responded: "Not so, Lord! Nothing common or unclean has ever entered my mouth!" Is this not an illustration of the Jewish mind-set in regard to touching and eating? Here is the "taste not" aspect of Torah set forth in powerful display!

Likewise, in Romans 14 where Paul is assuredly dealing with issues between Jews and Gentiles in regard to eating meats sacrificed to idols– doubtlessly with a Judaizing influence - he said in verse 17: "The kingdom of God is not eating and drinking, but righteousness and peace and joy in the Holy Spirit."

Why would Paul define the kingdom as *not* related to eating and drinking, within the context of Jew and Gentile controversy, if part of the controversy did not involve someone claiming that the kingdom is indeed defined by what a person eats and drinks– as under Torah? This corresponds perfectly with Colossians.

It must be kept in mind that while not many commentators take note of this, Paul's epistle (Colossians) is setting forth the restoration of Israel, the establishment of the Davidic kingdom. This is set forth powerfully when one examines chapter 1 and Paul's utilization of the Second Exodus motif, along with his discussion that God had translated the Colossians out of the power of darkness into the kingdom of His beloved Son. These are nothing more and nothing less than affirmations that Israel's eschatological hopes were being realized. This is the restoration of Israel.

It is important to conflate Paul's discussion of the kingdom in chapter one with Colossians 2:11f. In chapter 2, the apostle draws on several OT prophecies of Israel's last days restoration being the time when Israel would be circumcised in heart, not in the flesh. See Deuteronomy 30:1-10 / Ezekiel 36, etc. and Beetham's discussion of this (2008, 168+).

In spite of his earlier discussion of the kingdom, and how Paul was positing the restoration of the Davidic kingdom, Beetham perplexingly claims, "Israel's restoration is not the point at Col. 2:11" (2008, 174). He does, however, note that the restoration of Israel might have been, "the unexpressed implication of the apostle's thought." (174, N. 50). This is more than a little remarkable. As we noted above, nothing was more fundamental to Israel and *kingdom* than circumcision, Sabbath and Cultus. These tenets cannot be divorced from one another. Thus, the idea that in

Colossians 2:11 Paul does not have the restoration of Israel in mind is misguided. To restate: Kingdom and circumcision were inseparable tenets. To discuss one, was to discuss the other.

The New Moons, Feast Days and Sabbaths issue

There is little, if any dispute as to whether the elements listed in Colossians 2:16 have to do with Torah and the Judaizers The question that is important is, upon what basis do the commentators determine that we should essentially ignore these connections and look instead to a pagan source, a pagan problem at Colossae.

Some commentators have noted that other elements in Paul's discussion are indeed related to the Judaizing problem found in Paul's other epistles. O'Brien says: "Note Phil. 3:19 where Paul accuses his opponents of having their, "minds set on earthly things and making a god out of their belly, in contrast to those who citizenship in heaven." (Word Biblical Commentary, Colossians and Philemon, Vol. 44, (Waco; Word Publishers, 1982), 164). Is this not precisely what we find in Colossians 2? The correlations are impressive: affection on earthly things versus citizenship in heaven, attention to eating, and of course, earlier in Philippians 3, we find Paul addressing the issue of the true circumcision.

We might consider also Galatians 4 and Paul's discussion of the passing of Torah, the observation of "days, weeks, months and years" (Galatians 4:10)- and the *elements*. There, Paul speaks of the passing of "the elements of the world" (*stoicheia tou kosmou*) just as in Colossians 2:20 where he speaks of the passing of "the elements of the world" (*stoicheion tou kosmou*). The issues are directly parallel - Judaizers were imposing Torah but Paul tells his audience that those elements, that world, was to pass away. Consider something here.

If, as seems evident, Paul's referent to the passing of the "elements of the world" is an allusion to the passing of Torah, Cultus, and thus Temple, this adds to the dramatic effect of his epistle.

We would call attention to the fact that at the Jerusalem temple, the focus of the "New Moons, Feast days and Sabbaths," the veil of the temple had woven into it the "elements of the world."

Josephus and Philo agree that the four different colours from which the veil was woven represented the four elements from which the world was created: earth, air, fire and water. The scarlet thread represented fire, the blue was the air, the purple was the sea, that is, water, and the white linen represented the earth in which the flax had grown (Josephus, War 5.212-213).

Josephus adds:

> "The veils too, which were composed of four things, they declared the four elements; for the fine linen was proper to signify the earth, because flax grows out of the earth; the purple signified the sea, because the color is dyed by the blood of the sea

shell fish; the blue is fit to signify the air…; And for the ephod, it showed that God had made the universe of four (elements)… the breastplate was made to resemble the earth, the girdle represented the ocean, the Sardonxes the sun and moon, the twelve stones the months…" (Antiquities, Bk. 3, Chpt 7:7, p. 90) .

What this suggests is that the terminology of "the elements of the world," in Hebraic thought, pointed to the Temple and the cultus. So, for Paul to say that the elements of the world, the "New Moons, Feast Days and Sabbaths" were passing away, this was tantamount to a subtle, but powerful prediction of the impending destruction of the temple!

We must be reminded again of the interconnectedness between the tenets of circumcision, the Sabbaths, the festal observances, and the Temple- and the incredible importance of the Temple to the Jewish mind. Once again, it is difficult for the modern reader of scripture to grasp the significance of the temple to the ancient Hebrews. But, as Wright notes, to the Jews, "When you went up to the Temple, it was not *as though* you were 'in heaven.' You were actually there" (2013, 97+).

Gregory Stevenson points out the incredibly shocking nature of a prediction of the destruction of the temple and the end of the cultus - and the fulfillment:

"Destruction of the temple could be seen as tantamount to the destruction of the nation." (Gregory Stevenson, *Power and Place,* (New York; Walter De Gruyter, 2001), 168). He cites rabbinic sources who stated that with the destruction of Jerusalem and the temple, "an iron wall intervened between Israel and the Father in heaven." (p. 128). (See my *The Elements Shall Melt With Fervent Heat*, in which I document, from many sources, how fundamentally important the temple was in the mindset of the ancient Hebrews).

So, when Paul spoke of the passing of the elements of the world, there is good evidence to suggest that he was not speaking of the passing of the physical elements of material creation. He was focused on the fundamental elements of the life of Israel, Torah, Temple, Cultus and land.

As we have seen above in the comparison with Hebrews, there are many direct parallels between Paul's other epistles in which he is dealing with the Judaizers and Colossians.

We have in Colossians the contrast between the heavenly versus the earthly, which is found in Galatians, Philippians and in Hebrews.

We have the contrast - which we will not develop here - between *the flesh and the Spirit*. In both Galatians (chapter 3) and Philippians (chapter 3) is a direct contrast between the Judaizers and the things of Christ. And of course, we cannot forget the direct parallels between Philippians 3 and Colossians in regard to the issue of circumcision.

If the other contrasts and comparisons are accurate, it can safely be posited that in Colossians, we also have a contrast between two cities as we do in Galatians 4 / Philippians 3 and Hebrews.

In Colossians, from the first of the epistle to the last, Paul is laser focused on the fulfillment of Israel's eschatological hope. From his development of the Second Exodus, to his references to the kingdom, his echoes of numerous of Israel's Old Covenant kingdom / restoration prophecies (See Beetham's discussion of the Old Man versus the New, and his specific references to the focus of the debate in Colossae: circumcision, the Temple cultus - everything is related to the fulfillment of Israel's promises).

The regrettable oversight of the commentators to see Paul's focus has led to the suggestions noted above that he is engaged - at least to a degree - with a nascent Gnosticism, a syncrestic Judaism, or a hybrid Judaizing movement. In reality, Paul's adversaries at Colossae were the Judaizers, pure and simple. It is the identical situation as found in Romans, Galatians, Corinthians and Philippians. The Judaizers were seeking to impose Torah on the Gentile saints. They were imposing circumcision. They demanded observance of the Sabbaths. They were saying they had to offer the festal sacrifices. And that meant that they were telling the Gentiles that their hope - *their salvation* - was in the land where they had to offer those sacrifices!

Drawing Our Conclusion

In light of our discussion then, I believe that it necessary to take a fresh look at Colossians 3:1-2. When Paul told those Gentiles who were being pressured to put their trust in Torah and the observation of Temple praxis, to not set their minds on "the earth" he was not speaking of earth, *per se*. (By extrapolation one could make this application. Anything that would detract from Christ is wrong. But, "earth" is not Paul's *focus*). His exhortation to put their hope on "things above" is a contrast between the Old Covenant "land," the Old Covenant city, the Old Covenant Temple, and the heavenly realities of Christ! It should be seen in the context of the controversy at Colossians, which virtually all commentators agree, at least to some degree, was the Judaizing movement.

What is interesting is that, while I have found several commentators who honor the Judaizing nature of the controversy in Colossians, I have not found even one that comments on the issue of whether Colossians 3:2 should be "earth" or land. As noted at the first of this work, there are even some commentators that divorce Paul's exhortation in 3:2 from the controversy discussed earlier. But, I believe that this misses a critical element of Paul's controversy with the Judaizers. They were in fact setting their minds on "the land" and urging the Gentile saints to do the same. Everything they emphasized and sought to impose was focused on "the land" - the land of Israel. It is this that Paul

56

categorically rejects in Colossians 3:2.

The implications for seeing Colossians 3:2 within the context of the Judaizing controversy are profound for the modern Zionist / Dispensational doctrine. Paul was not simply giving a generic exhortation to be "heavenly minded" as suggested above by Robertson. *The apostle was rejecting the Judaizer's emphasis on Jerusalem, the Temple, the Cultus, the Land!*

This is a direct repudiation of modern Dispensationalism, because that school of thougt does *precisely* what the Judaizers were doing in Colossians, Romans, Corinthians, Galatians and Philippians. They were imposing Torah, the cultus, Temple and thus, "The Land" on the Gentiles.

We are told repeatedly that Israel has never possessed all of the land promised to her. This is fundamental to Premillennialism. Ken Gurley wrote: "At no time in Jewish history has Israel ever occupied all this land (see Deuteronomy 1:7; 11:24), and so, the nation of Israel will receive this promise in the future" (Ken Gurley, *Upholding Our Future Hope*, (HazelWood, MO; World Aflame Press, 2005), 198+).

Thomas Ice and Tim LaHay tell us: "The restoration of Israel in 1948 is the Super Sign of the end of the age" (Thomas Ice and Tim LaHaye, *Charting the End Times*, Eugene, Ore.; Harvest House, 2001), 119)." They say of that event, "Israel's re-gathering and the turmoil are specific signs that God's end-time program is on the verge of springing into full gear. In addition, the fact that all three streams of prophecy (the nations, Israel, and the church) are all converging for the first time in history constitutes a sign in itself." (p.84). (See my book, *Israel 1948: Countdown to No Where,* for a thorough refutation of this claim).

In the Dispensational / Zionist movement, *the physical land of Israel is the key to their eschatological paradigm.*

Dispensationalism says the land still belongs to Israel, and that the Davidic Kingdom will one day be re-established and centered in Jerusalem - and the land.

Dispensationalism says the Messianic Temple will be built in Jerusalem - in the land.

Dispensationalism says animal sacrifices in the Temple will be restored - in the land..

Dispensationalism says the cultic feast days will once again be observed - in the land.

Dispensationalism teaches the restoration of circumcision (Very reluctantly! They honestly do not like to discuss this issue, as evidenced in formal public debates that I have had). Without circumcision, there can be no worship in Jerusalem, the temple, the land.

Dispensationalism says that in the restored Davidic kingdom, if the nations refuse to travel to Jerusalem– i.e. in "The land" and worship at the Temple, with animal sacrifices, New Moons, feast days, and Sabbath observances, they will be cursed!

Thus, in every way, the very things that Paul rejected as central to the Messianic Kingdom and the salvation in Christ, is posited by the Zionist theology as essential to salvation and life in their proposed kingdom! And to reiterate, in the Dispensational paradigm, failure or refusal to obey will result in being accursed by the Lord.

Thus, In the Dispensational / Zionist movement, all believers are told that they must, *must*, put their affection on the land! *Focus is not on the heavenly things of Christ, but on the land!* (See my book, *The New Covenant: Future or Fulfilled?* for a more in-depth discussion of the Dispensational description of the Millennial kingdom. That book is available on Amazon, Kindle and from my websites).

We have the right to ask, therefore, what happens to the Gospel of Christ in the proposed Dispensational, Millennial, Davidic kingdom?

Paul's Gospel rejected physical circumcision ; Dispensationalism would re-instate it.

Paul's Gospel rejected observance of "New Moons, Feast Days and Sabbaths" - Dispensationalism would re-bind these things.

Paul's Gospel rejected animal sacrifices - Dispensationalism posits the restoration of what Paul negated.

Paul's Gospel identified the body of Christ as the True Temple to which the Old Temple pointed - Dispensationalism would rebuild that rejected Temple.

Dispensationalism flies directly in the face of Paul's teaching in Colossians! Paul said not to place affection on the land; Dispensationalism says our hope is on the land! There is something horribly wrong with a doctrine that says to do the very thing *that the apostle Paul commanded not to do!*

When Paul said, "do not set your minds on things on the earth / land" this is a powerful repudiation of everything Dispensationalism / Zionism stands for.

The challenge before the reader is to reject any and all emphasis on "the land," physical Jerusalem, the physical temple, and any form of a restored literal cultus. The invitation is for us all to set our minds on the things above - the fullness of Christ.

www.ingramcontent.com/pod-product-compliance
Lightning Source LLC
Chambersburg PA
CBHW060716030426
42337CB00017B/2896